T0358098

The Fox and the Crow

Retold and dramatised from the
Aesop's fable as a reading play
for partners or small groups.

Ellie Hallett

Ways to read this story

This story is suitable for school and home. Some 'how to read' ideas are below.

- With a partner or small group, take it in turns to read the rows.

- Don't rush! This helps you to say each word clearly.

- Think of yourselves as actors by adding lots of facial and vocal expression. Small gaps of silence also create dramatic energy. These techniques will bring the story to life.

- If you meet a new word, try to break it down and then say it again. If you have any problems, ask your teacher or a reading buddy.

- Don't be scared of unusual words. They will become your new best friends.
  (New words strengthen your general knowledge and enable you to become vocabulary-rich in your day-to-day life.)

Have fun!

Hungarian stamp, 1960 Public domain

Crow was sitting on the branch of a tree near an old farmhouse.

He was thinking about food.

At that very moment, he spotted something that made him fluff up his feathers with excitement.

It was a piece of cheese.

There it was, lying all by itself on the kitchen table, just begging to be eaten.

Crow started thinking deep thoughts.

'That piece of cheese looks to me as if it is unguarded.'

'If I'm quick, the farmer's wife won't see me.'

'I'll swoop down, grab it in full flight and disappear before she's any the wiser.'

And that is exactly what happened.

'Caw! That was the easiest snack I've found in a long time.'

'I'll now fly up and hide in amongst the cool leaves of this tree.'

'Eating is best enjoyed alone.'

'When I'm hidden from view, I'll be able enjoy my prize in peace and not be pestered by other birds.'

Crow didn't actually say any of these words out loud. He was too busy holding the cheese in his beak ...

… but these were more or less the thoughts he was thinking in his head.

'My next task is to find a branch where the leaves are the thickest.'

'I don't want any interruptions while partaking of this joyous morsel.'

And so Crow hopped from branch to branch to check which one was best.

While he hopped, he kept a firm grip on his newly acquired morning tea.

He wanted to make sure he couldn't be seen by those who might like to share his bounty.

And so he was very pleased with himself when he found the perfect spot.

'Ah - this will do nicely - high up and well hidden from prying eyes.'

'Now let me look a bit closer at what I have found.'

'Mmmm … It's quite firm, but oh, what a delightful smell!'

'And if I'm not mistaken - yes! It's a piece of rather lovely cheddar.'

'What a stroke of good luck, as I'm a bit peckish, you might say.'

'A tasty piece of cheddar will fit the bill perfectly.'

'Oh, what a lucky crow I am, and smart as well, I might add. My dear mother would be proud of me.'

Crow was just about to start nibbling on his piece of cheese when a smooth, golden sort of voice came up to him from under the tree.

'Why, hello Crow, my dear fellow!'

The voice sounded very pleased with itself, as if its owner was one of Crow's very best friends.

'Now I wonder who that could be! I thought I was alone, and suddenly I have company.'

'No matter.

I'll just ignore whoever it is and keep on with what I'm doing.'

Crow didn't say any of this out loud. We already know that his beak was fully occupied holding onto his cheese.

'My goodness, Crow. I've just this minute realised what a fine-looking, strong and glossy bird you are!'

Crow's curiosity got the better of him.

These words were impossible to ignore.

Crow peered down between the thick greenery of the tree with bright unblinking eyes.

He wanted to have a closer look at his visitor.

What Crow saw down below him there on the grass was a well-groomed and rather smartly turned out fox.

Fox was staring up at Crow.

'In fact, you are far better-looking than every bird in the district!'

'Oh yes! Even better-looking than White Swan who thinks she is a princess the way she glides up the river as if she owns the place!'

Fox kept looking up at where Crow was sitting in among the cool leaves.

Crow, of course, totally agreed with Fox.

He knew he was more qualified to be the centre of attention than Swan.

Fox had more to say on the subject.

'All White Swan does is paddle around in circles all day - and how silly is that?'

And there was a touch of contempt in Fox's voice as he described White Swan.

Crow kept looking down at Fox and Fox kept on looking up at Crow.

After a while Crow wondered if Fox was going to say anything more.

He liked being told how he was so good-looking and intelligent and handsome, and so on and so on.

Crow waited, his eyes big and wide.

He sat as still as he could, the cheese still securely gripped in his beak.

'Yes, Crow. Some may think Peacock is the most beautiful bird around here.'

'But my dear fellow - I disagree. Yes, I totally disagree!'

'You are far more eye-catching than Peacock with your glossy feathers.'

'That over-feathered show-off soon becomes very tiring to look at.'

'To my mind, Peacock's shimmering plumes have far too many colours.'

'Yes, *way* too many!

And he struts around here as if he was the king of the birds.

Huh!'

Crow shook his short and shiny black feathers as if to impress Fox even further.

He hopped down to a branch bathed in sunshine.

This enabled his wings to catch the morning light more easily.

Crow wanted Fox to have a better view of his beautiful black and shiny plumage.

'What a fine fellow that Fox is! Such good taste and refinement!

'After I eat my cheese, I'll be able to tell him how much I agree with him.'

Fox felt inspired to continue, and he spoke again to his willing audience.

'I have many friends in high places.

They all tell me how much they admire you, Crow.'

'Oh yes. They fully agree with me when I say that your wings are much longer and far stronger than Eagle's.'

'Oh yes, indeed, Crow, dear fellow! You should be very proud of your uncommonly noble wingspan.'

'And may I also say that you have a lot to crow about, dear chap!'

Crow puffed out his chest with pride at such flattering comments from Fox.

Crow imagined himself swooping past Eagle and he smiled to himself.

He was thinking of the surprised expression Eagle would have when Crow flew past her with such speed.

Crow kept looking down at Fox, and Fox kept looking up at Crow.

And then Fox became suddenly silent.

Crow decided it was probably now *his* turn to make the next move.

'I'll just pop down to a lower branch.'

'If I get even closer, it will encourage Fox to keep on speaking.'

'And what a charming fellow he is! I can't think why he has so few friends.'

Fox closed his eyes and sniffed the air.

At last Fox spoke again, but his voice was strangely much softer than before.

'Oh yes, my fine feathered friend. Another thought has just come to me.'

'Now that I've had time to consider it, you have even better eyesight than Hawk who flies so high.'

Crow puffed himself up again and made his eyes big and wide like Hawk's eyes.

What a kind and generous thing to say!

Crow imagined himself flying as high as the clouds and spotting a tiny mouse way down below.

He smiled to himself.

Hawk would shake his head in wonderment at Crow's ability to see something so small and far away.

Crow fluffed his feathers with pride.

Out of consideration for Fox's soft voice, Crow decided he should fly to an even lower branch.

This would enable the conversation to flow more easily.

Crow spotted a fine sturdy limb just above Fox's head.

He hopped down in happy anticipation.

'But!'

Crow almost fell off his perch.

Fox's voice was suddenly very loud. It was also quite sharp in tone.

'But, Crow, old boy.

What a shame you cannot sing!'

'Your voice is certainly *loud*, but that doesn't mean to say your voice is *good!*'

Crow blinked in shock and surprise.

He bent down to look at Fox.

He was still sitting just below him there on the soft green grass.

Crow gripped his cheese more tightly.

Crow had always regarded himself as being rather musically gifted.

Fox continued his speech in his loud and rather rude voice.

'All that talent, and yet you have missed out on the greatest splendour a bird can possess.'

'Ah, yes, it is a terrible pity that you don't have a beautiful singing voice!'

'Such a shame, especially when you have so many other fine qualities.'

Crow could contain himself no longer.

He'd show Fox that he did indeed have a beautiful singing voice, and this was the moment to show his talent.

Crow thought his voice was not only extremely loud, but was as melodious as any bird Fox might care to name.

Crow steadied himself on the branch, lifted his head and took a deep breath.

He opened his beak as wide as he possibly could.

'KWARK, KWARK! KWARK!'

'KWARK, KWARK!'

Crow gave his all to prove to the whole wide world that he could sing even better than a nightingale.

But of course, as soon as Crow opened his beak, that fine piece of cheddar started to fall.

Down it went, straight into the warm and waiting mouth of Fox.

With a triumphant look on his face, Fox caught the cheese like a champion.

Crow stared down at Fox in disbelief.

'Oh *no!* What have I done!'

**'My beautiful, delicious, magnificent piece of cheese has Gone!
Gone!'**

'KWARK!'

Fox stood up, he sat down. He turned around one way and then the other …

… all the while chewing with his mouth opening and closing.

Crow couldn't believe how easily he'd been tricked.

He realised now that Fox had planned how to take Crow's cheese from the moment he saw Crow fly into the tree.

'And that is why Fox has few friends!'

Crow shook his head, blinked his bright yellow beady eyes, and thought deeply about what had happened.

'I'm proud of what I have, but I know I will never be as good-looking as Swan.'

'I won't be as colourful as Peacock.'

'There is no way I will be able to fly faster than Eagle.'

'I will never have better eyesight than Hawk.'

'And, of course, Nightingale is by far a better singer than I will ever be.'

'But I *am* smart enough to know I won't be tricked like that again!'

As for Fox, he headed for the hills, still smiling and licking his lips.

And so whenever you hear a crow calling out **KWARK! KWARK** …

… in a loud and extremely unmusical voice …

… just remember the moral of this famous Aesop's fable …

Don't be tricked by flattery!

Milo Winter (1888 - 1956)

The Readers' Theatre series by *Ellie Hallett*

These **Readers' Theatre** stories have a major advantage in that everyone has equal reading time. Best of all, they are theatrical, immediately engaging and entertaining. Ellie Hallett's unique play-in-rows format, developed and trialled with great success in her own classrooms, combines expressive oral reading, active listening, peer teaching, vocabulary building, visualisation, and best of all, enjoyment.

ISBN	Title	Author	Price	E-book Price	QTY
9781921016455	Goldilocks and The Three Bears	Hallett, Ellie	9.95	9.95	
9781925398045	Jack and the Beanstalk	Hallett, Ellie	9.95	9.95	
9781925398069	The Fox and the Goat	Hallett, Ellie	9.95	9.95	
9781925398076	The Gingerbread Man	Hallett, Ellie	9.95	9.95	
9781925398052	Little Red Riding Hood and the Five Senses	Hallett, Ellie	9.95	9.95	
9781925398083	The Town Mouse and the Country Mouse	Hallett, Ellie	9.95	9.95	
9781925398014	The Two Travellers	Hallett, Ellie	9.95	9.95	
9781925398007	The Enormous Turnip	Hallett, Ellie	9.95	9.95	
9781925398090	The Hare and the Tortoise	Hallett, Ellie	9.95	9.95	
9781925398106	The Wind and the Sun	Hallett, Ellie	9.95	9.95	
9781925398113	The Three Wishes	Hallett, Ellie	9.95	9.95	
9781921016554	The Man, the Boy and the Donkey	Hallett, Ellie	9.95	9.95	
9781925398120	The Fox and the Crow	Hallett, Ellie	9.95	9.95	
9781920824921	Who Will Bell the Cat?	Hallett, Ellie	9.95	9.95	
9781925398021	The Ugly Duckling	Hallett, Ellie	9.95	9.95	

KNOWLEDGE
BOOKS AND SOFTWARE
PUBLISHING

www.kbs.com.au

Readers' Theatre